DOMINOES

Changing Places

STARTER LEVEL   **250 HEADWORDS**

OXFORD
UNIVERSITY PRESS

Great Clarendon Street, Oxford OX2 6DP

Oxford University Press is a department of the University of Oxford.
It furthers the University's objective of excellence in research, scholarship,
and education by publishing worldwide in

Oxford New York

Auckland Cape Town Dar es Salaam Hong Kong Karachi
Kuala Lumpur Madrid Melbourne Mexico City Nairobi
New Delhi Shanghai Taipei Toronto

With offices in

Argentina Austria Brazil Chile Czech Republic France Greece
Guatemala Hungary Italy Japan Poland Portugal Singapore
South Korea Switzerland Thailand Turkey Ukraine Vietnam

OXFORD and OXFORD ENGLISH are registered trade marks of
Oxford University Press in the UK and in certain other countries

First published in Dominoes 2004

2023

26

ISBN: 978 0 19 424708 5 BOOK
ISBN: 978 0 19 463912 5 BOOK AND AUDIO PACK

No unauthorized photocopying

Printed in China

This book is printed on paper from certified and well-managed sources.

ACKNOWLEDGEMENTS

Cover photograph reproduced with permission from: OUP (directors chair/Stockdisc).

Illustrations by: Thomas Sperling.

The publisher would like to thank the following for permission to reproduce photographs: Corbis pp ivc
(Leonardo DiCaprio/Kurt Krieger), ivf(Serena Williams/Duomo), 25 (Jeep in Mojave Desert/
Craig Aurness), 41 (Julia Roberts/Mitchell Gerber/AS400 DB); Getty Images pp39 (Newly-wed
car/Stuart McClymont), 40 (Penelope Cruz/Evan Agostini), 41 (Anna Kournikova/Martyn
Hayhow/AFP), 41 (Michael Schumacher/Jean-Loup Gautreu/AFP), 41 (Brad Pitt & Jennifer
Aniston/Kevin Winter), 41 (Tiger Woods/Scott Halleran), 41 (Will Smith/Kevin Winter);
OUP pp40 (Teenage girl/Photodisc); Rex Features p ive (Robbie Williams/Giuseppe Aresu);
Shutterstock pp ivd(Jennifer Lopez/Helga Esteb), 19 (Monument Valley/Sergey Yechikov),
32 (Monument valley/Julien Hautcoeur), 33 (truck/Paul Matthew Photography).

DOMINOES

Series Editors: Bill Bowler and Sue Parminter

Changing Places

Alan Hines

Illustrated by Thomas Sperling

Alan Hines is the author of *Square Dance*, a novel that he also adapted as a film starring Winona Ryder, Jane Alexander, Jason Robards, and Rob Lowe. He has published fiction and articles in a number of magazines in the United States and in Great Britain. In addition to *Square Dance*, he has written many other screenplays and movies for television, and his film *The Interrogation of Michael Crowe* won a Peabody Award. He has received many awards for his fiction, including the D.H. Lawrence Fellowship. He was born in Dallas, Texas, and now lives in Bucks County, Pennsylvania.

OXFORD
UNIVERSITY PRESS

BEFORE READING

1 Match the sentences with the pictures and tick the boxes.

	Movie Star	Zoo Worker
a It's exciting work.		
b It's different every day.		
c It's dirty work.		
d You can make a lot of money.		
e You can walk down the street and people don't look at you.		
f You don't make much money.		
g People always stop you in the street and want to talk to you.		
h It isn't very exciting.		

2 Would you like to change places with someone famous for a day? (They live your life and you live their life for 24 hours.) Who would you like to be? Why?

Jennifer Lopez

Serena Williams

Leonardo DiCaprio

Robbie Williams

Chapter one

This is Hal Tanner.

Every morning, Hal gets up at seven o'clock. He **feeds** Freddie, his dog. He eats his breakfast. Then he gets on his bicycle and goes to work.

feed to give things to eat to someone or something

Hal works at the **zoo**. He watches the visitors carefully. They can look at the **animals** – but they can't go near them or feed them.

Nothing changes from day to day. 'Nothing exciting happens in my life,' thinks Hal.

Sometimes at night, Hal has a wonderful **dream**. He is **famous** and he has an exciting life. Then he gets up in the morning and he is Hal again.

On the weekends, Hal meets Sophie. Hal wants to **marry** her soon.

---

zoo a place where you can see animals from different countries

animal a living being that moves; a dog or a cat is an animal

dream pictures that you see in your head when you are sleeping

famous when many people know about someone

marry to make someone your husband or wife

This is Tim Hawkins. Tim is a famous **actor**.

'I know that man,' people think, when they see Tim. They **stare** at him in the street. Sometimes they run after him. Tim does not have a **normal** life and he is unhappy.

For his next **movie**, Tim wears **glasses**. His face is very different in glasses. It's not Tim Hawkins' face and many people do not **recognize** him. Now Tim wants to wear glasses all the time.

actor someone who is in a film

stare to look at someone or something for a long time

normal usual, not different

movie a story that is on film

glasses you wear these in front of your eyes to help you see better

recognize to see someone and to know who it is

One morning, Hal gets up.
'Today isn't different from
yesterday or the day before that!'
Hal thinks. Then he remembers
something. In two days, he must
marry Sophie. He feels **nervous**.

When Hal gets to the zoo, a movie **crew** is
there. They are making a movie – with Tim
Hawkins! The crew are **filming**. Hal watches
for two or three minutes. He is very excited.

nervous a little afraid

crew a number of people who are
all working together

film to use cameras to make a movie

4

Later, Hal is eating a sandwich when Tim Hawkins walks in. Tim stares at Hal, and Hal stares at Tim.

'What!' Tim says. 'Who are you?'
'I'm Hal Tanner,' Hal says.
Tim looks at Hal and thinks for a minute. 'I have an **idea**, Hal Tanner. Let's have some **fun**. Let's change **places** for the afternoon.'

Hal thinks about this. Then he smiles. 'All right,' he says. He gives his **clothes** to Tim, and he takes Tim's clothes.

idea something that you think

fun something that you like doing and that makes people laugh

place where something is

clothes people wear these

READING CHECK

Match the sentences with the pictures and tick the boxes.

		Hal	Tim
a	He works in a zoo.	☑	☐
b	He's a movie star.	☐	☐
c	Nothing exciting happens in his life.	☐	☐
d	He wants to marry Sophie.	☐	☐
e	He's unhappy because he doesn't have a normal life.	☐	☐
f	He's making a movie at the zoo.	☐	☐
g	He watches the crew working on a scene.	☐	☐
h	He's eating a sandwich when the two men meet.	☐	☐
i	He says, 'Let's change places.'	☐	☐
j	He says, 'All right!'	☐	☐

WORD WORK

1 Complete the sentences with the words in the box.

> *famous* ~~*animals*~~
> *clothes   movies   actors*

a Cats and dogs are . . *animals* . . .

b Hats and shirts are . . . .

c The White House and Big Ben are . . . . buildings.

d *X-Men* and *Matrix* are . . . .

e Gwyneth Paltrow and Leonardo DiCaprio are . . . .

2 Use the words in the wordsnake to complete the sentences.

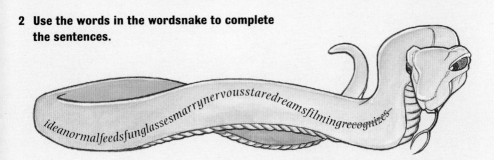

ideanormalfeedsfunglassesmarrynervousstaredreamsfilmingrecognizes

a Everybody recognizes . Tim Hawkins when they see him.

b People . . . . at him in the street.

c Every morning Hal . . . . Freddie, his dog.

d Sophie wants to . . . . Hal.

e Tim is . . . . in Hal's zoo one day.

f Hal has a very . . . . life.

g Hal has interesting . . . . at night.

h In his new film Tim wears . . . .

i Hal must marry Sophie in two days and he feels . . . .

j Tim has an interesting . . . . when he sees Hal.

k Changing places with somebody can be a lot of . . . .

GUESS WHAT

What happens in the next chapter? Tick two boxes.

a ☐ Hal is nervous before he starts to act.

b ☐ Hal isn't a good movie actor.

c ☐ Tim is a good zoo worker.

d ☐ Hal and Tim change back that evening.

Chapter two

Hal **brushes** his hair up.
Tim brushes his hair down.

Suddenly, a zoo worker comes in. 'It's time to go to work, Hal,' the worker says to Tim.

'This is easy!' Tim says. 'Who is Hal and who is Tim? Nobody knows.'
'Our mothers can't say, I'm **sure**!' Hal laughs.

brush to move your hair

sure when you feel that something is true

Everybody is looking at Hal now. At first he feels nervous.

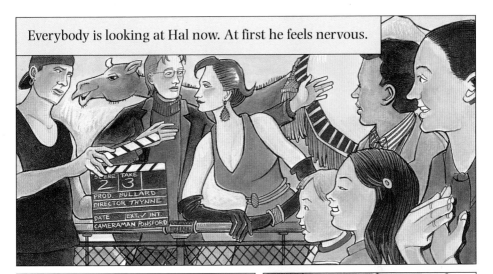

Soon, he is having fun. The crew loves the **scene**.
'You're wonderful!' they tell him.

Tim is happy, too.
'Good morning, Hal!' the zoo workers call to him.
Then Hal's **boss** comes to speak to him. 'Tanner, you must go to the **monkey** house,' he tells Tim. 'Can you work there for an hour, please?'

scene a part of a movie that happens at one time

boss a person who tells workers what to do

monkey an animal, usually with a long tail

Tim Hawkins lives an exciting life, Hal thinks.

Tim loves Hal's **job** because nobody recognizes him. This is a normal life, he thinks. And these monkeys are wonderful!

job work

Later, Hal and Tim meet. They must change their clothes again. Tim has many things to do that night.

'You are on a TV **talk show** at five o'clock,' Hal tells him. 'Then you have a **party** later.'

'I don't want to do those things!' Tim says. 'You do them. You be Tim Hawkins. You can do it!'

'I can be Hal Tanner,' Tim says. 'Let's do it for one more day.'

Hal feels afraid. But he's excited, too. 'OK,' he **agrees**. 'Let's do it!'

talk show when famous people answer questions on TV

party when people meet to have fun

agree to say 'yes'

READING CHECK

Put the sentences in the correct order. Number them 1–8.

a ☐ A zoo worker calls Tim 'Hal'.

b ☐ Tim goes to the monkey house.

c ☐ Hal and Tim agree to change places for one more day.

d ☐ Hal tells Tim about a TV talk show and a party that evening.

e ☐ Hal and Tim change their hair.

f ☐ Everyone looks at Hal in the movie.

g ☐ The crew says nice things to Hal.

h ☐ Hal's boss comes to speak to Tim.

WORD WORK

1 Find eight more words from Chapter 2 in the TV.

```
M O N K E Y S X J P
G C V A A G R E E A
B O S S A D S B I R
T B U F U B U O D T
X E I G J R R G E Y
L H D F A U E H A A
L H C I N S C E N E
J H A F K H I X Z G
J H U F X E S O P R
N X L P A S T Y J Y
T A L K S H O W J Y
```

2 Use the words in Activity 1 to complete these sentences.

a Tim doesn't want to be on a t a l k s h o w or to go to a p _ _ _ _ .

b Hal's b _ _ _ says to Tim; 'Go to the monkey house!'

c Hal and Tim b _ _ _ _ their hair up and down.

d Tim likes the m _ _ _ _ _ _ .

e Hal and Tim a _ _ _ _ to change for one more day.

f Hal likes Tim's j _ _ .

g 'Who is Tim and who is Hal?' says Tim.

'Our mothers can't say, I'm s _ _ _ !' laughs Hal.

h The crew loves the s _ _ _ _ with Hal in it.

GUESS WHAT

What happens in the next chapter? Tick two boxes.

a ☐ Freddie likes Tim.

b ☐ Hal doesn't like Tim's girlfriend.

c ☐ Tim likes Sophie.

d ☐ Tim helps when there is an accident in the zoo.

13

Chapter three

Hal tells Tim everything about Hal Tanner. He talks about his dog Freddie and his **girlfriend** Sophie. Tim tells Hal everything, too.

They agree to meet at an old building near Hal's house at six o'clock the next evening. Then they can change clothes again.

For Tim, this is easy. He has many different **roles** in movies.

Tim **tricks** some people, but he doesn't trick Freddie. 'Who is this man?' thinks Freddie. 'I don't recognize him. He's not Hal.'

girlfriend a woman that a man loves

role one of the people in a movie

trick to make people think that something is true

14

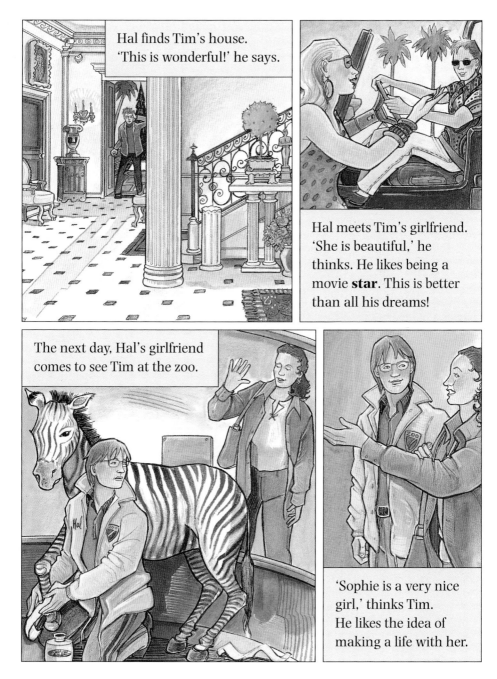

Hal finds Tim's house.
'This is wonderful!' he says.

Hal meets Tim's girlfriend.
'She is beautiful,' he
thinks. He likes being a
movie **star**. This is better
than all his dreams!

The next day, Hal's girlfriend
comes to see Tim at the zoo.

'Sophie is a very nice
girl,' thinks Tim.
He likes the idea of
making a life with her.

star a famous person

15

Being a movie actor helps Tim with Hal's job. Tim can **climb** very well because he makes a lot of **action** movies. There is an **accident** with the **sky tram** at the zoo and Tim climbs up to help the people in it.

In Hal's job at the zoo he works with people. He must be a **first aid** worker sometimes. Now, the film crew is filming an action scene in the **desert**. One of the crew has an accident and she isn't **breathing**.
'I can help!' says Hal, running to her.

climb to go up using your hands and feet

action where a lot of exciting things happen

accident something bad that happens

sky tram a train that travels high up

first aid giving help to people before a doctor can come

desert a place which usually has no water

breathe to move air in and out of your body

The people climb down from the sky tram. Tim helps them. 'I love climbing,' he thinks. 'And I love helping people.'

The woman is breathing again. 'It's fun to be a movie star,' thinks Hal. 'But it's wonderful to help people.'

READING CHECK

Match the big, black words with the people or things.

a 'I don't recognize him.'

b 'This is wonderful!'

c 'She is beautiful.'

d Tim climbs up to help the people in it.

e She isn't breathing.

f He likes the idea of making a home with her.

1 Tim's house

2 the sky tram

3 Freddie the dog

4 Tim's girlfriend

5 Sophie

6 one of the crew after she has an accident

WORD WORK

1 Find words from Chapter 3 in the dogs.

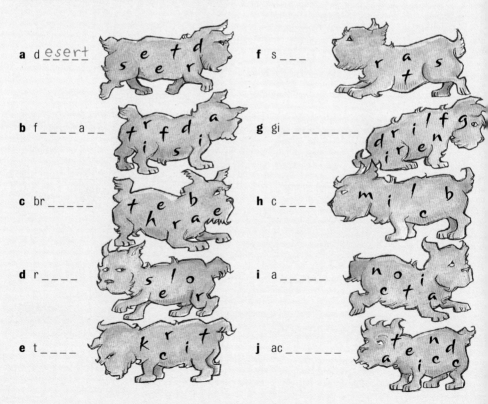

a d <u>esert</u>   s e t d s e r

b f _ _ _ _ a _ _   t r f d a t i s i

c br _ _ _ _ _   t e b h r a e

d r _ _ _ _   s l o e r

e t _ _ _ _   k r i t c i

f s _ _ _   r a s t

g gi _ _ _ _ _ _ _ _   d r i l f g i r e n

h c _ _ _ _   m i l b i c

i a _ _ _ _ _   n o i c t a i a

j ac _ _ _ _ _ _   s t e n d a i c c

2 Use the words from Activity 1 to complete the sentences.

a They are filming in the . . . desert . . . .

b Help her! She can't . . . .

c Tim is in lots of . . . . movies.

d Sophie is Hal's . . . .

e Tim can't . . . . Freddie the dog.

f Hal likes being a movie . . . .

g Tim has many different . . . . in the movies.

h Tim can . . . . very well.

i Hal sometimes does . . . . work at the zoo.

j There's an . . . . with the sky tram at the zoo.

GUESS WHAT

What happens in the next chapter? Tick the boxes.	Yes	No
a Hal and Tim change back again.	☐	☐
b Hal and Tim speak on the phone.	☐	☐
c Tim marries Sophie.	☐	☐
d The police run after Tim.	☐	☐

Chapter four

It is the evening before Hal's **wedding**.
Tim waits, but Hal never comes.

Tim waits for a long time.
He is getting nervous.

Tim goes back to Hal's house and calls
his **cell phone**. Hal has the cell phone
with him. But there's no answer.

wedding the time when two people
marry

cell phone a phone that you can
carry with you

20

Soon, David, Sophie's brother, comes to get Hal for the wedding **practice**.

Tim calls Hal again. Again, there's no answer.

Out in the desert, it is raining! The film crew cannot film in the rain. They all wait.

'I must leave,' says Hal. But nobody is listening to him.

practice when you do something before it happens because you want to do it well

At the wedding practice that evening, Tim must be Hal.

Tim is nervous at the practice **dinner**.

When nobody is looking, he leaves the room.

dinner when you eat a lot with lots of people on an important day

Tim goes to his house. He climbs over the **gate**. But the police see him. 'Stop!' they shout. 'Oh, no! I don't want anyone to see Tim Hawkins in these old clothes!' thinks Tim, and he runs away.

Usually, Tim runs from people. Now he is running from the **police**!

Tim **hides** from the police. There's nothing he can do. In twenty-four hours, he must marry Sophie!

gate a door in a garden wall

police men and women who stop people doing bad things

hide to go where no-one can see you

READING CHECK

Correct seven more mistakes in this chapter summary.

> evening
It's the ~~morning~~ before Hal marries Sophie. Tim waits for Freddie but he never comes.

Tim is getting nervous. He calls Hal, but Hal doesn't answer the door. Then Hal's brother,

David comes to get him. In the desert it's sunny. The crew waits to film. Everybody listens

to Hal when he says 'I must leave!' Tim leaves when someone is looking, and goes to his

house. But then the police see him there, and he must walk away from them.

WORD WORK

police
practice
hide
cellphone
dinner
gate
wedding

Use the words from the movie-making scene on page 24 to complete the sentences.

a When you have a . .cellphone. . you can phone people when you want.

b Before you do something important for the first time it's a good idea to have some . . . .

c The . . . . want to find the killer.

d My father's forty today and we're having a big . . . . for him tonight.

e Where can I . . . . ? I don't want people to find me.

f I can't go into the garden. The . . . . isn't open.

g Are you going to Tony and Sarah's . . . . ?

GUESS WHAT

What happens in the next chapter? Tick the boxes.

a Hal . . .

   1 ☐ leaves the desert with the film crew.

   2 ☐ leaves the film crew in the desert.

   3 ☐ phones Sophie.

b Hal takes Tim's Jeep and drives . . .

   1 ☐ to Tim's house.

   2 ☐ across the desert.

   3 ☐ to his wedding.

c Suddenly . . .

   1 ☐ Hal sees Freddie.

   2 ☐ the police stop Hal.

   3 ☐ the Jeep stops.

d Hal's cellphone rings. It is . . .

   1 ☐ Tim.

   2 ☐ Sophie.

   3 ☐ David.

Chapter five

The film crew is getting ready.
They are going to film a big scene.
'You don't understand,' Hal says.
'I must leave. It's very important!'

When nobody is looking, Hal leaves.

When the film crew runs after Hal, he hides. He wants to get back to Sophie. He must get back for his wedding.

27

Hal looks at Tim's **Jeep**.

'I can drive home across the desert in that,' thinks Hal.

In the dark, Hal walks carefully across to Tim's Jeep. Nobody sees him.

Hal gets in Tim's Jeep and drives away. He **disappears** into the night.

Jeep a small car that can drive where there aren't any roads

disappear to go away suddenly

Hal has no **map**. Soon, he is **lost**.

For a long time he drives here and there. He is looking for something that he recognizes. Then suddenly the Jeep stops. 'Oh, no! It needs **gas**!' Hal says.

Suddenly, Tim's cell phone **rings**.

map a picture that shows where things are, like streets, towns, rivers, or countries

lost not knowing where you are

gas gasoline or petrol; cars need this to work

ring the noise of a bell

It is Tim on the phone. 'Where are you?' Tim asks Hal. 'Why aren't you here?'

'I want to come back,' says Hal. 'But I'm lost. Where am I? Where are they filming the desert scene? Do you know?'

'No. I don't know!' says Tim. 'Someone always drives me to the filming in the morning and back home in the evening. But please get here quickly! I like Sophie, but I don't want to marry her!'

Suddenly, Tim's cell phone **goes dead**. 'Tim! Tim!' Hal cries.

go dead to stop working

'Oh, no!' thinks Hal. 'Today is my wedding.'

Just then, a **truck** arrives. There are **farm** workers in it.

The farm workers recognize Hal and they are excited. 'Look,' they say. 'It's Tim Hawkins!'

For a minute or two, Hal forgets all of his **problems**.

truck a kind of car for carrying things or people

farm a piece of land for animals or growing plants

problem something that makes you feel bad

READING CHECK

Correct the mistakes in these sentences.

a When the ~~police~~ _film crew_ run after Hal, he hides.

b Hal runs across to Tim's Jeep.

c He drives away into the hills.

d The Jeep stops slowly.

e Sophie phones Hal.

f When Hal asks 'Where am I?' Tim can tell him.

g Tim wants to marry Sophie.

h Some zoo workers take Tim in their truck.

WORD WORK

Use the words from the picture to complete these sentences.

farm   *lost*
gas   *map*
goes dead   *problem*
Jeep   *ringing*

a Hal drives away in Tim's ..... _Jeep_ ......

b 'The phone is .... Can you answer it?'

c 'Where are we? I don't know! We're ....!'

d 'The Jeep isn't working. It needs some ....'

32

e Suddenly the cell phone . . . . Hal can't call Tim.

f Good friends help you when you have a . . . .

g 'Can you see the next town on the . . . .? It's ten kilometres from here.'

h There were apple trees and lots of animals on the . . . .

GUESS WHAT

What happens in the next chapter? Match the first and second parts of these sentences.

a David, Sophie's brother . . .

b Sophie arrives . . .

c Tim says . . .

d Hal arrives . . .

e Sophie says . . .

f In the end Sophie . . .

1 in a wedding dress.

2 comes to get Tim for the wedding.

3 in the farm workers' truck.

4 'Which one of you is Hal Tanner?'

5 marries Hal.

6 'Stop everything!'

Chapter six

It is the day of Hal's wedding. The wedding **guests** arrive.

A lot of people are here for Hal and Sophie's wedding, and they are all **strangers** to Tim. David, Sophie's brother, comes to get him. 'It's time to go,' David says.

guest people that you ask to a wedding or a party

stranger a person you don't know

Tim and David go to the front of the **church** and stand there.

Sophie comes in when the **music** begins. She is beautiful in her wedding dress.

Just then, Tim says, 'Stop everything! This can't happen!'

church Christian people go here to pray

music people listen or dance to this

Everyone stares at Tim. Suddenly, they hear a truck, and then music. It's coming from **outside**.

The doors open, and Hal comes in with his new friends. The farm workers are playing music.

Sophie sees Hal. She looks at Tim, and she looks at Hal again. Then she **faints**.

outside in the open – not in a building

faint to fall down suddenly because something bad happens to you

When Sophie opens her eyes again, Hal and Tim tell her everything. The two of them are talking at once. 'Stop!' Sophie says. She gets up and looks at Hal and Tim. 'Which one of you is Hal Tanner?'

'I'm Hal,' Hal says. 'I'm sorry I'm late, but the desert is very, very big – and without a map, I–'
'Stop!' says Sophie, and she laughs. 'You're here now. That's the important thing.'
So, in the end, Sophie marries Hal, and Tim is a guest at the wedding.

Later, at the party, everyone is very excited to see Tim Hawkins, the famous actor. Of course, Tim likes that. Hal is happy, too, because he is with Sophie, and he can be Hal Tanner again.

READING CHECK

Write the sentences to make a summary of Chapter 6.

a [face] comes to get [face] for the wedding.

David comes to get Tim for the wedding.

b [face] is wearing a beautiful [dress] .

....

c Suddenly [face] says 'Stop everything!'

....

d Then people hear a [truck] through the window.

....

e The [church] doors open and [face] comes in with some [faces] .

....

f [face] feels ill when she sees [face] and [face] in front of her.

....

g In the end [face] marries [face] and [face] goes to the wedding.

....

ACTIVITIES

WORD WORK

Use the words from the picture to complete these sentences.

church   music

faints   outside

~~guests~~   strangers

a Lots of ....*guests*.... come to Hal and Sophie's wedding.

b All the people there are .... to Tim.

c Sophie and Hal marry in a ....

d When the .... begins, Sophie comes in.

e Sophie .... when she sees Tim and Hal in front of her.

f The people at the wedding suddenly hear the farm workers' music ....

GUESS WHAT

What happens after the end of the story? Choose from these ideas or add your own.

a ☐ Hal and Sophie go to see Tim's next movie.

b ☐ Hal and Sophie go to Tim's wedding.

c ☐ Hal writes a book: *Changing Places*.

d ☐ Tim makes a movie: *Changing Places*.

e ☐ Hal stops working at the zoo.

f ☐ ....

g ☐ ....

h ☐ ....

Project A   *Changing Places*

**1 Ana García is changing places with Penelope Cruz for a week.
Use the table to complete her 'Changing Places' project**

Ana García

Penelope Cruz

Usually . . .

- with my family in Valencia in Spain
- Spanish food
- go to school in the day
- do homework
- watch TV in the evenings

This week . . .

- in a hotel in Hollywood
- American food
- make a movie in the day
- meet lots of boys
- go to lots of parties at night

Changing Places

My name is Ana García. I usually live . . . .

. . . .

I usually eat . . . .

I usually go . . . .

I usually do . . . .

and . . . . in the evenings.

This week I'm changing places with Penelope Cruz.

I'm living in a hotel in Hollywood.

. . . .

. . . .

. . . .

2 Now choose a famous person and fill in the table for you and them.

	Your life	Your famous person's life
where/live?		
what/eat?		
what/do every day?		
what/do evenings?		

3 Use your table to write a 'Changing Places' project.

Changing Places

My name is . . . .

I usually live . . . .

I usually eat . . . .

I usually go . . . .

I usually . . . .

. . . . in the evenings.

This week I'm changing places with . . . .

. . . .

. . . .

. . . .

Project B — *Describing a scene*

1 **Here is a scene from Tim Hawkins' latest movie – *Desert Dog*. In the movie Tim Hawkins is Bron Pearson – a famous policeman. Write the verbs correctly to complete the description.**

In this scene Bron **a)** .is visiting.. *(visit)* the zoo with the beautiful Russian policewoman Raissa Guliyeva. They **b)** . . . . *(look)* at a desert dog in the zoo. It **c)** . . . . *(have)* a big mouth and long legs and it **d)** . . . . *(be)* a killer. At the moment it **e)** . . . . *(sit)* under a tree and **f)** . . . . *(sleep)* in the sun. In the movie desert dogs **g)** . . . . *(be)* important and expensive animals. There **h)** . . . . *(not be)* more than five in the world today. Behind Bron and Raissa we **i)** . . . . *(can)* see the zoo boss – Zach Ponsonby – a very bad man. He **j)** . . . . *(want)* to sell the desert dog to a Bolivian zoo. The boss of the Bolivian zoo **k)** . . . . *(talk)* to Mr Ponsonby on his cellphone. A little girl – Trudy Goodshoes – **l)** . . . . *(stand)* next to Mr Ponsonby, and she **m)**. . . . . *(listen)* to him.

PROJECTS

2 Look at the pictures and complete the sentences with the words in the box.

> across away from behind in in front of
> into next to on over through under

a Hal is sitting . . . . his bicycle.
Freddie is . . . . him.

b Hal is sitting . . . . Tim's jeep.
He is driving off the road and . . . .
the desert.

c Sophie is standing . . . . Tim.
Hal's brother is . . . . them.

d Freddie is . . . . the table and
Tim is coming . . . . the door.

e The sky tram is going . . . . the zoo.
The truck is driving . . . . the zoo.
Some people are walking . . . .
the zoo.

3 Here is another scene from the movie *Desert Dog.* Write a description.
Use the words in the box to help you.

> afraid box driver hungry plane tree

In this scene Zach Ponsonby . . .

GRAMMAR

GRAMMAR CHECK

Adverbs of frequency

We use adverbs of frequency, such as always, usually, often, sometimes, and never, to talk about how often we do something. Adverbs of frequency usually come before the main verb but after the verb be. *Hal is sometimes bored.*

always	*Hal always gets up early.*
usually	*Hal usually eats a sandwich for lunch.*
often	*Tim often meets famous people.*
	Tim sometimes wants to have a normal life.
sometimes	*Exciting things never happen to Hal.*
never	

1 Choose the correct words to complete the texts about Tim and Hal.

People a) **often**/never recognize Tim in the street because he's a movie star. They stare at him, and they b) **always**/**sometimes** run after him, too! Tim isn't happy when people do that. Tim c) **never**/**always** meets normal people because all of his friends are famous, and he d) **often**/**never** stays at home in the evenings because he goes to TV talk shows and parties. Tim's life is e) **never**/**usually** very exciting, but he isn't happy. He f) **often**/**never** wants to live a normal life.

Hal g) **often**/**always** gets up at seven o'clock because he starts work at eight. He h) **always**/**sometimes** goes to work on his bicycle because he doesn't have a car. Hal is i) **sometimes**/**usually** very tired after work because there are a lot of animals at the zoo, but he likes his job. After work he j) **often**/**always** meets his girlfriend Sophie, but he doesn't see her every day. Really exciting things k) **sometimes**/**never** happen to Hal, but he l) **sometimes**/**never** has a wonderful dream at night. In the dream he is famous, but then he wakes up, and he is Hal Tanner again.

GRAMMAR CHECK

Have: affirmative and negative

We use **have/has** (for *he*, *she*, and *it*) to talk about possession.

I have an idea.

Hal has the cell phone with him.

To form the negative, we use **don't/doesn't** (for *he*, *she*, and *it*) + have.

Tim doesn't have a normal life.

To make questions, we use **do/does** (for *he*, *she*, and *it*) + have. We reuse the auxiliary verb in the answer.

Do you have a girlfriend, Hal? Yes, I do.

2 **Write sentences with the correct affirmative or negative form of *have*.**

a Tim / a dog called Freddie. *Tim doesn't have a dog called Freddie.*

b Sophie / a boyfriend ....

c Tim / a jeep ....

d Hal and Sophie / famous friends ....

e Tim / a beautiful girlfriend ....

f Hal / a job at the zoo ....

g Sophie / glasses ....

h Hal and Tim / dark hair ....

i Hal and Sophie / a normal life ....

j Tim / a brother called David ....

k Hal and Sophie / big houses ....

3 **Write questions and short answers.**

a Tim / an exciting life?

 Does Tim have an exciting life? *Yes, he does.*

b Sophie / a role in Tim's new film?

 ....

c Tim and Hal / blue eyes?

 ....

d Hal / a bicycle?

 ....

GRAMMAR

GRAMMAR CHECK

Modal auxiliary verbs: must

We use must + infinitive without *to* to talk about strong obligation.

In two days, Hal must marry Sophie.

Later, Hal and Tim meet. They must change clothes again.

4 **It's the night before Hal's wedding. Who must do these things? Use some of the people more than once.**

Tim	the farm workers	Hal	Tim and Sophie
	Tim and Hal	Sophie	the film crew

a act in Tim's film

.... *Hal must act in Tim's film.* ....

b run from the police

....

c wear a wedding dress

....

d leave the desert

....

e phone Hal

....

f change their clothes again

....

g go to a wedding practice

....

h take Tim's car

....

i film a big scene with Hal in the desert

....

j arrive at the wedding in time

....

k drive Hal to the church

....

Verb + infinitive or –ing form

We use the gerund (–ing form) after verbs, such as *finish*, *go*, and *love*.

Let's finish filming this scene.

We use the infinitive with *to* after these verbs: *want*, *would like*, *need*, *forget*, *remember*, and *learn*.

Hal wants to marry her soon.

We can use a gerund or infinitive with *to* after some verbs, such as *like* and *begin*.

I like helping people.   *I like to help people.*

5 Match the parts of the sentences. Who says these things? Write Hal or Tim.

a I like *helping people.*   ☐ 10 *Tim*

b I love being …   ☐ ………

c I can go …   ☐ ………

d I want to wear …   ☐ ………

e I need to …   ☐ ………

f Sometimes I would like …   ☐ ………

g I love …   ☐ ………

h I don't want anyone …   ☐ ………

i Don't forget …   ☐ ………

j I like Sophie, but …   ☐ ………

k I can't leave before they …   ☐ ………

l Remember …   ☐ ………

1 arrive at the church on time.

2 glasses all the time because people don't recognise me.

3 living in Tim's house.

4 to meet me tomorrow near my house.

5 to have a normal life.

6 driving in Tim's jeep.

7 finish filming the scene.

8 to feed my dog Freddie.

9 to see me in these old clothes.

10 ~~helping people.~~

11 a famous movie star for a few days.

12 I don't want to marry her.

GRAMMAR CHECK

Indefinite pronouns: people and things

We use indefinite pronouns to talk about people and things when we don't say who or what exactly. The ending –one means the same as –body.

people	things	
someone/somebody	something	*Somebody recognizes Tim – Freddie!*
no one/nobody	nothing	*Tim loves Hal's job because nobody recognizes him.*
everyone/everybody	everything	*Hal tells Tim everything about Hal Tanner.*

6 Choose the correct words to complete the texts.

Hal wants to leave the desert. He tells a) **no one/everybody** in the film crew, 'I must leave.' But b) **nobody/someone** listens to him so he takes Tim's jeep. c) **Everyone/Somebody** looks for Hal, but they can't find him. Later, Hal is driving through the desert. 'I don't recognize a thing!' he thinks. Suddenly the jeep stops because it needs gas. Hal is late for his wedding, and he can do d) **nothing/something** about it. But then he sees e) **nothing/something**. It's a truck. Maybe f) **nobody/somebody** in the truck can help him?

Normally g) **no one/everyone** knows Tim because he's a famous movie star. But now he's got Hal's hair and Hal's glasses, and h) **somebody/no one** recognizes him. He's standing in the church and i) **everybody/nothing** is looking at him. He can't marry Sophie: he must say j) **something/everyone** quickly. Suddenly he shouts 'Stop k) **everything/someone**! This can't happen!' l) **Everyone/No one** stares at him because they don't understand. Suddenly they hear m) **everything/something** outside the church. n) **Someone/Nobody** opens the door. It's Hal … or is it?

GRAMMAR CHECK

Possessive forms

We use possessive adjectives to talk about possession.

I	my
you	your
he/she/it	his/her/its
we	our
they	their

Hal brushes his hair up.   *She is beautiful in her wedding dress.*

We use 's and ' to talk about possession with nouns and names.

We use 's with singular nouns and plural nouns without –s, and ' for most plural nouns.

Tim – Tim's house is very big.   *monkeys – Tim is working in the monkeys' house.*

We can use 's or ' for singular nouns and names ending in –s.

Tim Hawkins – Tim Hawkins' new movie is called Desert Dog. ✔

Tim Hawkins – Tim Hawkins's new movie is called Desert Dog. ✔

7 Complete the text with the correct possessive form.

Sophie can hear the farm workers a) .....?..... music. When she opens b) ....

eyes, two men c) .... faces are staring at her. But which one is d) ....

boyfriend Hal, and who is e) .... new friend?

Hal tells f) .... girlfriend all about Tim and g) .... adventure together.

'But I don't understand,' says Sophie. 'Tim Hawkins doesn't wear glasses.'

'I know,' says Hal. 'Tim is wearing h) .... glasses.'

'But where are i) .... wedding clothes?'

'Tim's wearing j) .... clothes and these are Tim k) .... clothes,' says Hal.

'But why are you late for l) .... wedding?'

Hal tells Sophie all about m) .... drive through the desert in Tim n) .... jeep.

'Well, you're here now. That's the important thing,' says Sophie. 'And welcome to

o) .... wedding, Tim! Come and meet p) .... brother David.'

'I know q) .... family,' says Tim. 'Remember the wedding practice last night...!'

GRAMMAR CHECK

Question words

We use question words, how, what, when, where, which, who, and why in information questions.

Why are you wearing those old clothes?

Where does Hal live?

Which one of you is Hal Tanner?

Who does Tim change places with?

8 **Complete the questions with the question words in the box and match them with the answers. Use some question words more than once.**

Where	Which	How	What	Why	When	Who

a ..When.. does Tim go to the wedding practice? `[4]`

b .... do Hal and Tim want to change places? ☐

c .... does Hal usually work? ☐

d .... does Hal think about Tim's life? ☐

e .... recognizes Tim in Hal's clothes? ☐

f .... does Hal leave Tim's jeep? ☐

g .... does Hal get to the wedding? ☐

h .... happens when Sophie sees Hal and Tim? ☐

i .... person does Sophie marry? ☐

1 Hal leaves it in the desert.

2 It's really exciting.

3 She marries Hal.

4 The night before Hal's wedding.

5 Because they want to have some fun.

6 She faints.

7 In a zoo.

8 Hal's dog, Freddie.

9 Some farm workers drive him to the church.

DOMINOES Your Choice

Read *Dominoes* for pleasure, or to develop language skills. It's your choice.

Each *Domino* reader includes:
- a good story to enjoy
- integrated activities to develop reading skills and increase vocabulary
- task-based projects – perfect for CEFR portfolios
- contextualized grammar activities

Each *Domino* pack contains a reader, and an excitingly dramatized audio recording of the story

If you liked this *Domino*, read these:

A Pretty Face
John Escott
Zoe Baker works in a bookstore. She also likes acting, and she has a part in the play Romeo and Juliet. Mike Morrison writes about the play for the newspaper. What does he write about Zoe? Is Zoe a good actress ... or is she just 'a pretty face'?
What does Zoe think when she reads the newspaper? What does she do?

Blackbeard
Retold by John Escott
The year is 1717. It is a bad time to be the captain of a ship in the Caribbean because of pirates. The most frightening pirate on the sea is Edward Teach, or 'Blackbeard'.
'The Governor of Virginia wants us all dead!' Blackbeard thinks. 'But can he kill me – the most famous pirate in the Caribbean? No!' This is his story...

	CEFR	Cambridge Exams	IELTS	TOEFL iBT	TOEIC
Level 3	B1	PET	4.0	57-86	550
Level 2	A2–B1	KET-PET	3.0-4.0	–	390
Level 1	A1–A2	YLE Flyers/KET	3.0	–	225
Starter & Quick Starter	A1	YLE Movers	1.0–2.0	–	–

You can find details and a full list of books and teachers' resources on our website:
www.oup.com/elt/gradedreaders